The Haunted Mansion AFTER DARK

The Unauthorized Guide to the (Genuine) Grim Grinning Ghosts

50th Anniversary EDITION

This book is a reprint of the
"Haunted Mansion" chapter*
from the book
"The Park After Dark:
The Original Unauthorized Guide to
the Happiest (Haunted) Place on Earth"
by
Richard Carradine

(*with additional material)

**BY GHOSTLY DECREE
THIS SPOOKY GUIDE
BELONGS TO...**

_____

Cover Art and Interior Illustrations by
Richard Carradine

ᴛʜᵉ Haunted Mansion AFTER DARK

The Unauthorized Guide to the (Genuine) Grim Grinning Ghosts

50th Anniversary EDITION

This book is a reprint of the
"Haunted Mansion" chapter*
from the book
"The Park After Dark: The Original Unauthorized Guide to
the Happiest (Haunted) Place on Earth"
by
Richard Carradine

(*with additional material)

GHOULA Press - Los Angeles
www.ghoula.org

GHOULA Press
www.ghoula.org

For my Bride, Angela.

CAUTION:

Disneyland and its Haunted Mansion are living experiences and, as such, specific elements of the attraction mentioned in this book are subject to change without notice, and may not be available during your next visit to the park. Please accept this book as a unique snapshot in time.

Table of Contents

Note to Reader:

Clarification of terms: There is an apocryphal story that when Disneyland was built and needed to be staffed, Walt Disney created terminology for his employees that mirrors the entertainment industry as a way to avoid hiring minorities. Thus, under this logic, he could exclusively hire the "all-American" teenager (white) he envisioned to populate his fantasy world under the guise that he was "casting" parts, and not filling positions. Occasionally, an African-American, Latino, or Asian worker may slip through but they would be "cast" for Adventureland, Frontierland, and Tomorrowland, respectively. But, under no circumstances would these ethnic "cast members" be allowed "on stage" against the back-drop of "Main Street."

Whatever the truth is behind Disney's initial invention for these titles, the terms still very much exist today (without the alleged discrimination) at every level. The following is a list of words that are used throughout the book, and their definition as it relates to Disneyland.

Guest - customer
Cast Member - employee
Costume - uniform
On Stage - the area accessible to the customers.
Back Stage - the area where only employees are allowed
Attraction - ride

In addition, inside this humble book, terms such as ghost, apparition, spirit, entity, phantom, and manifestation are all meant to define a paranormal experience, and are interchangeable. Although there have been attempts elsewhere to draw differences between these words, as of yet there are still no universally accepted distinctions. So, for the sake of simplicity, this book does not adopt any of those subtleties.

"We're out collecting the ghosts,
and we're making it very attractive to them,
hoping that they'll want to stay at Disneyland."
---Walt Disney

WARNING:

Some of the supernatural stories described in this book may be unsettling to certain readers. The tales herein are presented and intended as entertainment or information. There is no intent to emphasize any particular belief, philosophy or religion.

"We'll take care of the outside,
and the ghosts will take care of the inside."

---Walt Disney

Introduction

I like ghost stories. I collect ghost stories like other people collect stamps. I love tracking down new ones. It's like hunting for buried treasure, because people are always reluctant to share these stories with strangers. People tend to laugh off my questions about ghosts, claiming there are no such things. But after some prodding, even the most cynical non-believer will point me towards someone who has a story. The skeptics always say, "I personally have never seen anything, of course, but you should talk to..." and so it goes. These stories (like all folklore) are passed down from person to person, as part of an oral tradition, where each teller breathes new life into the tale.

I grew up in a household where the subject of Disneyland came up frequently at the dinner table. My father was an Imagineer with almost three decades of experience working for "The Mouse House." My mother was one of two "Snow Whites" handpicked by Walt Disney for the 1964 World's Fair in New York. I, myself, at age 13, was cast by Walt Disney Imagineering to portray "Tomorrow's Child" for a filmed sequence to be projected during the finale of the Spaceship Earth pavilion at EPCOT Center.

My likeness was featured prominently in the attraction for many years. Later, as a teenager, I had the good fortune to work in various capacities at many of Disney's theme parks and studios on both coasts of the United States.

This book, therefore, represents the combination of two of my favorite topics of conversation. That is, ghost stories and Disneyland. So, it was only natural that I would one day write this book based on all of the stories I have heard, and collected, from fellow Cast Members over the years during my numerous trips through the Magic Kingdom.

This collection, however, of ghostly yarns about Disneyland, by no means represents a definitive study of the subject. It is just my simple attempt to retell the tales I have been told in the hopes that these stories will continue to live on and be passed down further.

Is there any truth in these stories? Did these people actually see what they described? Is Disneyland really haunted? Who knows? I leave it to the reader to decide what to make of the information presented in this guide. They can dismiss these stories as pure rubbish. They can take them at face value as stories. Or, they can believe all of them or part of them as the truth. Do I think these stories are true? I don't care either way.... I just like ghost stories.

Richard Carradine
President
GHOULA
Los Angeles, 2010

Foreword

It is hard for me to remember a time before the yellow tracing paper. And the brown pencils. The ritualistic unrolling of the new plans and the subsequent makeshift weights to hold down the corners. These are touchstone memories of my childhood. Recalling them place me immediately to a time, a place.

For 28 years, my father was the VP, Executive Concept Architect for Walt Disney Imagineering. Our home was a playground and a landing pad for the visuals of his plans and his work. I can also recall countless concepts that for one reason or another never saw the light of day and disappeared like a ghost. Of course I can walk through the parks to this day and point to my father's work (as well as the places his work could have been).

Now, my kid memory seems to recall a time when Las Vegas was trying to rebrand itself as a family destination with whimsically-themed hotels and amusement park-like attractions. Of course this meant there was elevated chatter in the house about WDI exploring the idea of a Disney resort there. Playing off the surrounding desert, it was to be Christmas-themed. It would evoke Santa's North Pole. Everything would be covered in show even the pool's water slides (made to look like ski slopes), and wait for it, a "Nightmare Before Christmas" themed casino inspired by the Oogie Boogie sequence. Jack and Sally would also dominate the inside of the hotel.

Well, what we all know now is that Las Vegas dropped the family-friendly idea in the desert dust and created the "What happens in Vegas, stays in Vegas." campaign.

However, like most of the ideas shared at home that never happened, some pieces survived and were reworked into other areas. The snow-themed water slides were lifted from their seasonal surroundings and placed in Florida to became Disney's Blizzard Beach.

I can't help but feel that the "Nightmare Before Christmas" takeover of the Haunted Mansion has something to do with the momentum that was built behind the Las Vegas plans, concept art, and ideas that weren't meant to die. As Jack Torrance felt in the Overlook Hotel, so too did I when I first rode through the Nightmare/Mansion mash up. Like I'd always been there. This was an idea that had been chewed on and mulled over for some time throughout my childhood and left abandoned in various ways, and yet here it was alive and well. It would be important to note now that these dream-like memories are washed with the innocence of my childhood.

That yellow tracing paper was the fabric of my youth illustrating the stories I would get to tell so many years later beyond the electricity of those living room walls. I imagine Walt himself might have wanted imaginations to flourish and be fostered in this way. And I'd like to think he would enjoy the real cobwebs and real ghosts that have come to call his Haunted Mansion home. Spiced up every year by an idea horrifying enough to have almost had a chance in Las Vegas.

Caitlyn Carradine
Atlanta, 2019

Caitlyn Carradine is a costume designer and founded The MudLArk Co., a custom design and apparel company, which serves film, television, and live performances. She is also the author's sister.

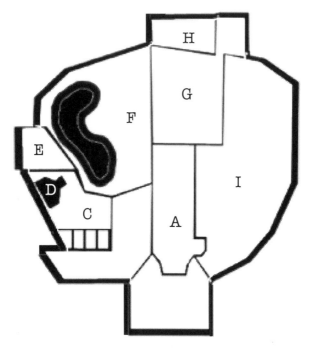

Disneyland

A.) Main Street
B.) Adventureland
C.) New Orleans Square
D.) The Haunted Mansion
E.) Critter Country
F.) Frontierland
G.) Fantasyland
H.) Mickey's Toontown
I.) Tomorrowland

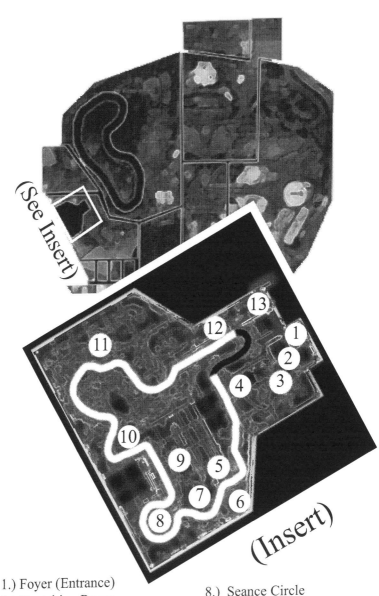

1.) Foyer (Entrance)
2.) Stretching Room
3.) Portrait Corridor
4.) Load Area
5.) Endless Hallway
6) Conservatory
7.) Corridor of Doors

8.) Seance Circle
9.) Grand Hall
10.) Attic
11.) Graveyard
12.) Crypt (Load Off)
13.) Little Leota (Exit)

1951 concept for a "haunted house" at Disneyland near Main Street with a graveyard next to it. (Never built.)

1957 concept for a "haunted house" at Disneyland for Frontierland near the Jungle Cruise. (Never built.)

The realized "Haunted Mansion" in New Orleans Square built in 1962 and opened to the public in 1969.

The "house" sits on the site of previous attractions Holidayland, Magnolia Park, and the Indian Village.

NOTICE!

All Ghosts And Restless Spirits
Post-lifetime leases are now available in this
HAUNTED MANSION
Don't be left out in the sunshine! Enjoy active
retirement in this country club atmosphere - the
fashionable address for famous ghosts, ghosts trying
to make a name for themselves... and ghosts afraid to
live by themselves! Leases include license
to scare the daylights out of guests visiting
the Portrait Gallery, Museum of the Supernatural,
graveyard and other happy haunting grounds.
For reservations send resume of past experience to:
Ghost Relations Dept. Disneyland
Please! Do not apply in person.

(From a sign placed at the entrance years before
the Haunted Mansion was open to the public.)

When hinges creak in doorless chambers, and strange and frightening sounds echo through the halls; Whenever candlelights flicker where the air is deathly still - that is the time when ghosts are present, practicing their terror with ghoulish delight!

Welcome, foolish mortals, to the Haunted Mansion. I am your host, your... ghost host. Kindly step all the way in please and make room for everyone. There's no turning back now...

Our tour begins here in this gallery where you see paintings of some of our guests as they appeared in their corruptible, mortal state...

Your cadaverous pallor betrays an aura of foreboding, almost as though you sense a disquieting metamorphosis. Is this haunted room actually stretching? Or is it your imagination, hmm? And consider this dismaying observation: This chamber has no windows and no doors, which offers you this chilling challenge: to find a way out! Of course, there's always my way...

The following chapter
has been reprinted from the book
"The Park After Dark: The Original Unauthorized
Guide to the Happiest (Haunted) Place on Earth"
by
Richard Carradine

(for more info go to page #97)

Haunted
Haunted Mansion?

The idea of a classic "Haunted House" attraction at Disneyland seems to have always been a part of Disney's land, even if it wasn't fully realized until 14 years after the park's opening (and 3 years after Disney's death). As if it were cursed, this project kept getting delayed, shelved, and reworked from the very beginning. Even after the house itself was finally built, it was a few years before the doors actually opened to the public. This led to many rumors that behind the locked gates, the mansion was indeed haunted.

It is said that even the janitors that worked in the offices of the Imagineers developing this ride were so unnerved by the gruesome concept art that they were afraid to set foot in the rooms where the Haunted Mansion drawings, models and plans were kept. Interestingly, the logo for Walt Disney Imagineering is Mickey Mouse dressed as he appeared in the "Sorcerer's Apprentice" sequence of Fantasia with his magic wand and wizard hat, both of which are traditional symbols of the occult.

One of those early conceptual pieces (that frightened the janitors), the model that was used to explain to Walt Disney the "Pepper's ghost illusion" a centuries old magic trick, used in the "ballroom scene," has left those "scary" offices and is now included among the amazing collection of magic memorabilia at Hollywood's Magic Castle, a club house for professional magicians (and a former Victorian mansion) which fittingly is also said to be very haunted.

In addition, Walt, himself, told fellow employees (Imagineers and Cast Members) that he truly believed the Haunted Mansion building was actually haunted, but then again Disney was a master of promotion, and knew the value of a good ghost story.

Originally this Disneyland attraction was to feature its own fictional ghost story about a wealthy sailing merchant, who built this antebellum home for his young bride. The story, which also involved an old well with something hidden at the bottom, was to gradually unfold during the attraction.

As this tale goes, once the happy couple moved in, she discovered the dark secret that his wealth was obtained by his exploits as a blood-thirsty pirate. Confronted with this unforgivable information, he flew into a fit of temporary insanity, and murdered his wife. When he regained his wits, and saw what he had done, his overwhelming guilt drove him to suicide. Ever since those events, the sad spirits of two star-crossed newlyweds wander the halls.

Although the Sea Captain story was created for this attraction (perhaps as a way of connecting this attraction to the Pirates of the Caribbean), only a few elements from it ever made it into the ride, most notably, the bride in the attic, the ghost ship changing portrait, and the ship weather vane at the very top of the house, which can be seen from the entrance.

Shades of this original yarn were also reworked into Walt Disney's 1977 movie, "Candleshoe," starring a young Jodie Foster. Ironically, this film adaptation did not include the ghosts of the original 1953 book.

Although, people don't generally associate Southern California with pirates, there is a surprising amount of pirate lore (and legends of buried doubloons) in its history. The story of one of Los Angeles' most colorful pioneers bares a striking resemblance to the Haunted Mansion's original pirate narrative, even if it is most likely coincidence. Miguel Blanca (aka Michael White) had a sorted past of piracy and smuggling before he married, settled, and became a prominent member of society (even becoming a judge). Strangely, even the well outside his house is also connected to a dark tragedy, the death of Kathy Fiscus.

In that early pirate-themed concept for this attraction, guests would be led through the house by a tour guide. Along the way, the guests would encounter a disembodied voice that would speak directly to them called "The Lonesome Ghost." As this walk-thru evolved into a dark ride, the human guide was eliminated and the idea of the ghostly voice was expanded (or possibly the two parts were merged), and eventually given the new name the "Ghost Host."

While Disney's designers were working on the early version of this now famous ride, were they influenced by something happening in a small North Hollywood studio a couple of miles away? Was the "Lonesome Ghost" a reference to the local radio personality, who went by the on-air alias, "The Lonesome Gal?"

One has to remember that in the 1950s, "The Lonesome Gal" was a wildly popular late-night radio show that was heard on more than 400 radio stations across the country. The secret to the show's success was a simple gimmick.

Between musical interludes, the nameless "Lonesome Gal" (portrayed by actress Jean King) would whisper sexy/suggestive non-sequiturs, speaking into the microphone as if she were talking to her lover. Lonely males would listen to her program and daydream that she was talking directly to them. To avoid men stalking her (and to create a little mystery), Jean King wore a black mask when appearing in public to promote the show or the show's sponsor.

Given that the early "Lonesome Ghost" version of the Haunted Mansion was developed during the height of her "Lonesome Gal" fame, the "lonesome" moniker for the mostly voice-only character (who addressed the tour directly) seems more than coincidental. Although there have been many reasons given for the elimination of the "Lonesome Ghost," one little discussed possibility is the very litigious nature of Jean King, who would threaten lawsuits to anyone trying to capitalize off the character she created.

The building where those historic radio programs were recorded (as well as the upstairs apartment used by Jean King) still exists today, and it is said to be haunted, namely disembodied voices have been heard by the current (and past) tenants.

In a strange case of the after-life imitating art imitating life, could the "Lonesome Gal" now be a "Lonesome Ghost" like the one she inspired?

That early original incarnation of the attraction was supposed to feature a special effect in which the Sea Captain's wet, dripping body would vanish before the Guest's eyes, leaving a puddle with wet footprints leading away from where he stood seconds before.

As a side note, there is a ghost story attached to Walt Disney World in Florida that is very similar to the Sea Captain's disappearing trick. A man wearing a wet pilot's uniform has often been spotted in a backstage administration building. Obviously seeing a man in costume backstage at Disney World is not too unusual even if he is wet. However, this pilot would vanish into thin air, leaving a puddle and wet footprints behind.

Over the years, Walt Disney World security guards received so many calls about this phantom that they keep a file on these strange occurrences. Then, a reference to this phantom appeared in a Halloween edition of an in-house newspaper for WDW Cast Members called "Eyes and Ears." This started a company-wide discussion of the sightings, and prompted the security team to look into the subject more thoroughly (perhaps it was a homeless man secretly living inside the building). It became the first sanctioned "ghost hunt" on Disney property. Ultimately, it was revealed that during the construction of that building a skeleton and pieces of a vintage aircraft were pulled out of the marshland at that very location. Again, could this be a case of life (or after-life) imitating art?

Fictional pirate backstories aside, as you approach the entrance to this "Southern plantation" house, its fun to think about the building's possible inspiration.

Architecturally, we know that the facade's design was based on a photo of the long gone Shipley-Lydecker house of Baltimore. This connection to Baltimore is telling, considering how much the works of former Baltimore resident, Edgar Allan Poe, clearly influenced the early concepts for this dark ride.

Although most of the Poe moments (Po-ments?) never left the drawing board, there is still elements left over from that phase, namely the presence of the raven throughout this dark ride (like Poe's "The Raven"), who in one version of the script was the ride's narrator. Other Poe motifs (Po-tifs?) like premature burial, walled in bodies, and echoing heart beats are found in other Poe stories.

"Spook houses" have always been a staple of amusement parks, however Walt Disney clearly did not model this attraction on any of the traditionally themed scary dark rides from other amusement parks. Instead, he turned to an actual "haunted mansion" (and tourist trap) for inspiration, the famous "Winchester Mystery House," located in San Jose, California (just up Interstate 5 from Disneyland).

Perhaps the séance room with a female medium at the heart of this attraction is an ode to Sarah Winchester's daily communications with the spirit realm at the heart of her very own haunted mansion.

By the way, Mrs. Winchester's haunted mansion also features a chamber that seems to have no doors, and no apparent exit once you step inside. Tour guides often pose the same "chilling challenge," to find a way out to the visiting tourists, just like in Disneyland's Haunted Mansion

Mrs. Winchester also had a fascination with the number thirteen (not unlike Disney), which may be the reason Guests are taken down an odd non-linear hall with too many doors (not unlike the real Winchester Mystery House) and are shown the number 13 just before they enter the séance room.

However, these similarities aside, there is another authentic haunted house that seems to have more in common with Disney's Mansion than even the famous Winchester Mystery House. Known as "one of America's most haunted homes," the Myrtles Plantation sits in Louisiana not far from the real New Orleans (just as Disney's Haunted Mansion is situated away and outside of their fake New Orleans).

Although the uniquely regional architecture bears some comparison to Disney's Louisiana-themed Haunted Mansion, the true similarities lie in the ghostly inhabitants. The Myrtles Plantation's dark history involves a birthday party with a poisoned birthday cake, a Voodoo Priestess that was hanged from a chandelier above the parlor, as well as a former resident that was killed in a duel.

In addition to the many ghosts that roam the halls and knock on the doors of this cursed house, witnesses claim to see a candelabra that floats up stairs and down halls, as well as a piano that plays itself. All of these elements can be seen today in Disneyland's Haunted Mansion.

The doomed birthday party is seen in the "ballroom." The Voodoo Priestess appears in "portrait corridor" as the changing "cat lady," (an enchanting skill Voodoo Priestess' are said to have). There is a hanged skeleton over the "stretching room," which appeared in promotional material as a woman's skeleton (with a dress and big fashionable hat). The duel is reenacted every few seconds in the ghostly portraits over the "Ballroom." The floating candelabra is seen in the "endless hallway," and the "knocking" phenomena mentioned is in the "corridor of doors."

Ken Anderson, one of Disney's favorite artists and Imagineers, traveled throughout the south visiting plantations to research this attraction. So, most likely these spooky similarities aren't just coincidences.

As a side note about the previously mentioned changing Voodoo "cat lady" portrait, in recent years the cat portion has been altered from a black panther (of traditional Voodoo folklore) to a tiger. The tiger is now in line with other recent alterations in the attraction, involving a murderous bride and her husband-victims. In earlier generations a "Tiger Woman" (or a "Tigress) was a newspaper euphemism for a woman who kills.

As another side note about the previously mentioned floating candelabra, it may have a deeper meaning than just a reference to the ghosts of the Myrtles Plantation. It could be a reference to a certain kind of ghost known as a "Will-o-wisp." Although there are many versions of the phenomenon, and every continent in the world has its own folklore surrounding its appearance. It is said to be a flickering light in the distance from possibly a torch, or a lantern, or candles.

In some cases, it is a spirit either guiding you to, or away from, a hidden treasure. Its fun to think about the idea of there being a lost treasure hidden inside the walls of the Haunted Mansion, if only it could be found. Could it be all the ill-gotten gains from the former pirate of the early narrative of the story of the Haunted Mansion? These ghostly lights are also known to lead travelers, either to safety or into peril. It seems fitting that the floating candelabra is the first spirit we encounter once we enter our "Doom Buggy."

Is its materialization indicating that we will have safe passage through this haunted house, or is it foreshadowing our impending doom.

The title of this Disneyland attraction is Disneyland's most accurate since it also is the most haunted. Over the years, there have been many stories about ghosts harassing Guests in this attraction. Unfortunately, there are also many tales of Cast Members, taking advantage of the spooky environment and the darkness, and fooling with unsuspecting Guests as well. So, separating fact and fiction is often difficult.

Disneyland fanatics are quick to point out that this ride doesn't really have the 999 happy haunts as promised (if you count each special effect and animatronic figure). However, it could be argued that, from a story stand point, Guests traveling through the Mansion are led to the attic, where they are promptly hurled backwards out the window (either by accident or by foul play) to their death below only to end up wandering the graveyard with the other ghosts.

Not only do you exit the ride, up and out, through a crypt (as if a ghost leaving the grave), but this idea may be foreshadowed even before you enter the house when the line redirects you to walk past other outside crypts. In the stretching room, when it appears that the Guests are trapped with no way out, the narrator says "of course there is always my way...," which is followed by breaking glass and the scream of someone falling to their death. Are those sound effects meant to reveal the only true way to escape (out the window)?

Is the implication that at least some of the 999 happy haunts are the other Guests that have gone before you, who met their demise? Is this why there is the ominous invitation to become the 1000th Guest? ("Any volunteers?").

Is that why the ride vehicles are called "Doom Buggies?" Are they leading you to your doom (as suggested earlier by the floating candelabra discussion)? The subtle implication that the Guest's own death is part of the story can also be found in dark rides elsewhere in the park.

Nine-hundred-ninety-nine or not, it would appear Disneyland's Haunted Mansion does have at least 13 actual ghosts...

1.) First of all, a few years back a video clip appeared on the world wide web, claiming to show a ghost at this popular attraction. The clip shows a collection of surveillance screens capturing a transparent figure "walking" from the entrance of the attraction down the walk way towards the Rivers of America.

Every couple of years, when this video resurfaces to a new audience, it is always followed by the explanation of "video burn-out." One can find a full debunking, technical description of this online, but even still many believe there is a ghost (some have suggested its Walt Disney, himself) haunting the entry to the mansion making that eternal nightly walk.

2.) There is the formal ghost of a man dressed in a tuxedo, complete with a top hat. He is often thought to be a costumed Cast Member working at the ride until he mysteriously vanishes into thin air.

Often, a Cast Member will see him out of the corner of their eye or reflected on a surface as if it were approaching from behind. Thinking he is another Cast Member coming to take over the next shift, they'll turn to greet him, only to find no one there.

A variation to this story has the man coming face to face with the Cast Member, trying to tell him/her something, but no sound comes from his moving lips.

3.) During the construction of this attraction, the chatter of people talking was heard coming from inside one of the walls in what is now the "séance room." Assuming the voices were emanating from a pocket transistor radio that was accidentally placed inside the wall, a worker poked holes in the wall in an attempt to find it.

When the source of the strange sounds could not be found, he simply repaired the wall and placed the ride's speakers at that spot to drown out the noise. So, as your "doom buggy" passes through, listen carefully, you may hear the real voices from beyond, trying desperately to make contact.

Along those lines, late at night, when the attraction is closed to guests, Cast Members over the years have heard the distinctive sound of children's laughter. When the Cast Member tries to track down the source of the giggling, they can never find it. As they travel from room to room. It always sounds like it is coming from the next room, or just around a corner, leading that person on an endless chase around the Haunted Mansion. At least these "children" are happy, unlike some other children said to haunt here...

4.) In addition to the séance room's unearthly chatter, Cast members have claimed to have experienced other strange phenomena in this room, such as phantom hands touching their arms as they walk through.

An often repeated urban legend explains the ghostly activity in this room as being connected to a teenager (possibly drunk) who climbed out of his "doom buggy" to explore this darkened room on foot. Unaware of a deep gap in the unlit floor, he fell and broke his neck, dying on the spot.

5.) Like the curiously creepy hands of the seance room, there is other gruesome grabbing going on earlier in the ride. One former Cast Member tells a story about the area just before the "endless hallway." In an earlier era of the ride, mischievous teens and kids would attempt to jump out of the "doom buggy,' and try to touch the floating candelabra, and race back to their vehicle before it had moved on to the next scene.

To discourage this unruly behavior, a Cast Member was stationed in a tiny hidden alcove, against the wall, at the top of the "stairs" just before the "endless hallway," where they could instantly step out in to the scene to stop any shenanigans. One day, a Cast Member walked up to his position, and backed into the space (which only has room for one person).

In the darkness, he felt a hand drop on to his shoulder, as if someone were behind him, already occupying that narrow spot. He apologized, and turned to greet what he thought was his co-worker, until he realized the alcove was empty, and there wasn't even room for anyone else to fit.

What's interesting about this ghostly experience is that it mirrors an idea in one of the early incarnations of this attraction. At one point, when the Haunted Mansion was a group tour led by a guide, there was to be a hairy arm that would suddenly appear from a hidden door and attempt to grab the guide. It was a simple scare, based on a scene from the classic film "The Cat and the Canary." Apparently, although that gag never made it into the attraction, there appears to be an arm of another sort doing the same thing.

6.) Cast Members have sworn that sometimes they hear the sounds of a fist knocking coming from inside the funeral carriage placed in front of the building's façade. With regard to this carriage, it should be pointed out that white hearses were historically used for the funerals of children or babies.

7.) There is a story that the suit of armor towards the beginning of your tour, has been known to move inexplicably, beyond the rigged shaking, to actually step forward towards the Doom Buggy. Unfortunately, these tales might not have anything to do with ghosts. For a brief time, the Walt Disney Company experimented with having a costumed Cast Member (in a suit of armor) wander the ride and try to startle Guests as they passed. Legend has it that this tactic was too scary, so it was removed from the ride.

Some versions of that story further explain that a Guest was so frightened by the suit of armor that she had a heart attack and died. Is this a case of an actual event being distorted into a ghost story, or has the emotional torment (and possible subsequent death) of that event scarred this attraction forever?

So, even though that costumed Cast Member no longer walks the halls, could residue energy of those encounters still linger?

8.) At the exit ramp as one leaves the ride, a miniature figure of a ghostly bride known by employees and fans as "Little Leota" usually beckons Guests to "Hurry baaaaack!," however some Cast Members claim that they have heard her break from the pre-recorded spiel and address those Cast Members directly, sometimes calling out their names.

9.) There is a female passenger that over the years has only been seen by the surveillance cameras. She appears clearly in the security monitors, but when her Doom Buggy reaches the end of the ride at the unloading area, it is always empty. Perhaps she doesn't wish to leave the ride just yet. For this reason, she has been nicknamed the "1000th happy haunt."

A similar phenomenon occurs elsewhere in this attraction with children. Could these separate ghosts be connected? Perhaps it is a worried mother eternally moving around, searching for her lost child(ren).

10.) Also, there is the ghost known simply as "the man with the cane." He has been seen after hours hobbling as if lost or disoriented. When a Cast Member approaches to help, he vanishes into thin air.

It is often repeated that this elderly spirit died of a heart attack. Death by heart attack has, over the years, been attributed to just about every ghost haunting in this attraction, as well as a few elsewhere in the park.

The problem with the heart attack aspect of the story is that, as stated earlier, there is an urban legend that the Haunted Mansion was originally so scary that one of the early Guests actually died of a heart attack during the ride. Shortly there after, supposedly, the effects were toned down.

So, it is possible that all these ghosts have been wrongly attributed to this urban legend. Likewise, confused storytellers may have mixed up scenes (or even attractions). Then again, maybe it is all true.

However, the most curious aspect of this apparition is that he has also been spotted at the Haunted Mansion at the Magic Kingdom in Walt Disney World. Whether, both Haunted Mansions are haunted by the same ghost, or similar ghosts, or that this is just the result of confused or misinformed story tellers is unknown.

11.) In a twist on the will-o-wisp ghosts mentioned earlier, Cast Members have claimed that show lights that are in a fixed position will suddenly move, and illuminate a different area of the room, and then after a moment, just as quickly, they will move back into their proper position.

Generally, the Cast Members will think it's maintenance making an adjustment, or someone playing a joke, until they realize there is no way to reach the light fixture without a ladder.

Perhaps the spirits are trying to make their presence known by moving these objects like Madame Leota commands the spirits to do in the seance room.

12.) There is also a story about a little girl that is sometimes seen in the Ballroom. Because of her ghostly transparent nature she is often mistaken for one of the many animatronic "apparitions" in that scene, and goes unnoticed.

However, the hardcore fans of the ride are puzzled by her occasional appearance, since they know that she is not part of the sequence, and when they go through the attraction a second time, she is absent. So, keep your eyes open as you pass through this part of the show, because if you are lucky you may see a real spook.

13.) The last ghost also seems to have a duplicate elsewhere. Cast Members, who work the "load off" area, helping people out of their Doom Buggies and onto the moving sidewalk will sometimes see a boy crying to the side where guests are not supposed to stand. After a moment, he vanishes. Some even claim that this crying boy even appears on the security video monitors, even though no one is actually there.

The story passed down as to the origin of the "crying boy" is identical to that of the "boat boy" in the "Pirates of the Caribbean," where a mother illegally dumps the ashes of her deceased child inside the ride. Could this same event have happened twice? It's certainly possible. Did one mother spread half of the ashes on one ride, and half on another? It's also possible. Or, has this story been mistakenly attributed to one of the ghosts as an explanation?

Speaking of explanations... There are a few theories as to why this Haunted Mansion in Disneyland is such a magnet for spiritual activity.

Some religious Cast Members believe that the "999 Happy Haunts" is an inverted allusion to the number 666, otherwise known as the mark of the devil, and thus an invitation to the dark side of the spirit realm like the shadow of the clawed hand that appears over the demonic clock inside the ride.

Speaking of invitations, before the Haunted Mansion was opened to the public, there was an invitation posted in front of the building for ghosts to take up residence there. Even earlier, while Walt Disney was traveling through Great Britain, he supposedly told the press that he also was there trying to convince some of London's famous ghosts to move to Disneyland's new haunted house attraction.

Some people believe all that beckoning, and inviting, does tempt the spirit world to act. This is the same idea behind séances (and the seance room).

On a more humorous note, there was also a children's book published when Disneyland opened that told the story of an angry leprechaun that lived on the land before it became Disneyland. As the story goes, the construction for the park forced him out of his tree stump home. When Mickey Mouse realized this, they offered to build him a new house inside Disneyland, but the tiny green-suited man refused. Instead, the leprechaun moved into a secret location where he could continue his mischievous antics.

It has been jokingly suggested that this little prankster is behind the strange occurrences in the Haunted Mansion, since there is inexplicably an audio animatronic leprechaun in the graveyard scene of the ride.

At this point, it should be noted that for Disneyland's 50th anniversary, Imagineers decided to actually recreate the leprechaun' house as it appeared in the illustrations in the book, and it can now be found hidden among the bushes in Adventureland.

That said, most legitimate theories have to do with what was on this spot before they built the mansion.

In 1957, Walt Disney fulfilled one of his life-long dreams of having his own circus. Though mostly forgotten today, the circus' "big top" tent was placed approximately where the Haunted Mansion stands today. Could the mistreatment of animals that was so common in these unregulated shows be the reason for the psychic sadness that gravitates to this spot, or do the origins of the phenomena go further back?

There is a legend that the land under the Haunted Mansion is cursed, and possibly all of Disneyland, itself, may also be cursed.

The Haunted Mansion was erected on the spot very close to another Disneyland attraction that was eliminated years before, the "Indian Village."

According to the legend, on the last day of that attraction's existence, the "Indians" that were hired to entertain the tourists with folk dances of their culture cursed the ground. Some have even suggested that they performed the infamous "Ghost Dance."

This ancient folk dance was used by tribes of the old west to (as they believed) summon the spirits of their fallen ancestors, make the white man disappear, and restore their way of life.

Why would Disneyland "Indians" do this? Was it out of anger for the stereotypical way that their people and customs were depicted elsewhere in the park? Or, were they just unhappy about losing their jobs? We may never know.

In addition to whatever these Native Americans may or may not have done, there is speculation that the land is cursed not by these "Indians," but by ones over a hundred years ago, because it is thought Disneyland was built over a forgotten Indian burial ground.

This notion that the park is cursed is also rooted in another legend surrounding the Haunted Mansion. The Haunted Mansion is located roughly next to the place that the Dominguez ranch house originally stood. In this tale, when the Dominguez family sold their family farm to Walt Disney to build his amusement park, as part of the deal they made Walt promise that he would never tear down the old farm house that had tremendous sentimental value to the family. As a member of a farming family, himself, Disney understood this family's attachment to their home.

Although original conceptual art for Disneyland placed a "haunted house" attraction in the exact spot of the Dominguez family Ranch House, Disney kept the rustic farm house and put the "haunted house" idea on the back burner. Walt, true to his word, left the old home standing, using it as administration offices, and built his Disneyland and all the attractions around it.

However, after Walt died, the building was lifted and moved "backstage" where it was eventually, and unceremoniously, torn down. Cast Members believe this broken promise accounts for the spiritual unrest in the Haunted Mansion.

The idea of a "Disneyland Curse" is often evoked when talking about the numerous mishaps during the televised opening day ceremonies at Disneyland. There were so many operational problems that first day that it was nick-named "Black Sunday" within the company. Some have even tied Robert Kennedy's assassination to the "Disneyland Curse," since he visited the park in the days before he was fatally shot in nearby Los Angeles.

Incidentally, Robert Kennedy (also a possible victim of the "Kennedy Curse") has been attached to other famous curses, including the "Rosemary's Baby Curse," since he also visited the ill-fated director of that classic horror film, Roman Polanski, days before his assassination.

Because of the demonic themes explored in the film, "Rosemary's Baby," it is believed that those connected to this satanic film, invited tragedy into their lives. This is not unlike those who believe the devilish depictions inside the Haunted Mansion may be the reason for the attraction's spiritual unrest.

Coincidentally, Polanski's wife, actress Sharon Tate (who is also said to be a victim of the "Rosemary's Baby" curse) was slain as part of the infamous "Manson Murders" that shocked the world on the same day that the Haunted Mansion officially opened to the public.

Strangely, the next day, the "Manson Family" murdered a couple, who had lived in one of Walt Disney's former homes.

Interestingly, another victim of the "Rosemary's Baby Curse," William Castle, the famous horror film director, who produced "Rosemary's Baby," and who suffered health problems after the cursed movie's release, also has many strange connections to the Haunted Mansion, as well as Disneyland, itself.

Although filmmaker William Castle worked in all genres throughout his career, he is most fondly remembered for his horror films.

It's easy to draw comparisons to Alfred Hitchcock, because both filmmakers excelled in the area of suspense, and both were larger than life personalities, who created on-screen personas that introduced their work with gallow's humor.

However, one can also point out the similarities between Castle and Disney, who also had very dark elements in his family faire, and also cultivated a likeable persona hosting his TV shows.

Both Castle and Disney targeted the same young audiences, and at times Castle's film's (like his "The Spirit is Willing' or "13 Frightened Girls") felt like they could have been made at the Disney Studios. William Castle's "Zotz!" (similar in tone to Disney's "Absent-Minded Professor") was a book that Disney had wanted to adapt into a movie, but Castle had already secured the film rights.

Like Disney (and Hitchcock), William Castle is easily one of the most influential directors of the 20th century, inspiring a generation of horror writers like Stephen King, and film auteurs like George Lucas and Steven Spielberg, who in turned begot the generations after them (as well as some other attractions at Disneyland and Disney-like attractions else where).

Beyond that, the impact of Castle's showmanship can also even be felt at Disneyland, and more specifically the Haunted Mansion...

It is known that Walt Disney took his Imagineers to see William Castle's "13 Ghosts" (1960) for inspiration and ideas for their haunted house project.

Castle created a gimmick for this campy classic called "Illusion-o," where audience members received a "ghost viewer" to make ghosts appear or disappear, depending on which colored filter you look through.

Not only did Disney's creative team experiment with ghosts that change color, but some of the concept art of that period are scenes pulled straight out of the movie like an early idea involving a ghostly lion.

The movie also uses the term "haunted mansion." Is this why Disney changed his "haunted house" project to the "haunted mansion?"

The poster for the movie even featured a woman hanging from a noose that is almost identical to an image from Haunted Mansion promotional material.

Also one could argue that the dueling spirits coming out of the paintings in the ballroom scene is straight from the ending of "13 Ghosts."

There is also the conceptual issue of a place where ghosts have been gathered from around the world like the collection in "13 Ghosts," or as the Haunted Mansion's Ghost Host says "There are several prominent ghosts who have retired here from creepy old crypts all over the world."

Walt Disney also encouraged his designers to look at other horror films of that era for ideas. Although, "The Haunting" (1963) has been often cited as the inspiration for the "warping door" sequence in this ride, there is another classic "haunted house" film directed by William Castle of that era, that also seems to have had an influence on the attraction.

"House on Haunted Hill" (1959), which was directed by William Castle, was the first film to be presented in "Emergo," a gimmick that was supposed to make the action jump off of the screen.

In reality, at a key moment during the movie, a fake skeleton was dangled over the audience to evoke fright, exactly like the skeleton dangled over the Guests in the Haunted Mansion's "stretching room." So, it seems William Castle's creation of "Emergo" is still alive and well, half a century later, scaring tourists everyday at Disneyland. Somewhere, William Castle's ghost is smiling and laughing.

However, there are other interesting similarities between the Haunted Mansion and "The House on Haunted Hill." The "house" of "House on Haunted Hill" coincidentally also had an inexplicably clean and well-maintained exterior juxtapositioned against its abandoned, dusty haunted interior. (Incidentally, that "house" lives on as well as the Frank Lloyd Wright inspired restroom over in the Hollywood Backlot area of Disney's California Adventure).

Also, at one time Disney's "haunted house" was going to be a part of a never built project called "Riverfront Square" in St. Louis. It was to be elevated on a mound and become the focal point of the park upon entry (like the castle is to Disneyland). The haunted house on top of the hill was to be called appropriately "Haunted House Hill," which coincidentally sounds like the title of Castle's film "The House on Haunted Hill."

There was also a phase in the building's development, when artist Sam McKim was involved, where the house reflected more of a Spanish/Caribbean style.

There was a pagoda-like tower featured at one end of a long building. This early design, before the familiar facade of today, bore a striking resemblance to the house featured on the poster for "The House on Haunted Hill," which oddly looked nothing like the actual house used in the movie.

On a minor note, related to Castle's possible influence on the development of the Haunted Mansion, one of the paintings in the "stretching room" looks almost identical to a moment from Castle's dark comedy, "The Old Dark House" (1965).

There is also a scene in "The Spirit is Willing" (1967), where a ghost sits on a chandelier like in the Haunted Mansion's ballroom scene. Incidentally a ghostly Sea Captain is featured heavily in that film, not unlike the early draft of the Haunted Mansion's show.

Plus, Paul Frees, the man responsible for the spooky narration ("The voice of the Haunted Mansion") previously provided similar spooky narration for Castle's horror films.

In a fun twist on art imitating life imitating art, when "The House on Haunted Hill" was remade in 1999, the main character, originally played by Vincent Price, was reworked into a man who creates theme-park attractions. Was this a nod by the filmmakers to acknowledge the influence that movie and William Castle had over Disneyland?

In addition to the Haunted Mansion, it appears that Disney (or his Imagineers) may have copied another classic William Castle gimmick over in Tomorrowland.

The devices that made the seats rumble inside the now long gone "Flight to the Moon" (known previously as the "Rocket to the Moon," later rethemed "Mission to Mars") attraction look surprisingly similar to William Castle's "Percepto" devices. This was a gimmick he used in his film, "The Tingler" (1959), that also made theater seats vibrate when a large bug-like creature attacked its victims (including some unsuspecting members of the audience). Interestingly, collectors have attempted to track down these unique pieces of movie memorabilia, but all the "Perecepto" devices seem to have disappeared. Did Disney. or the Disney Company, buy all of them to use at Disneyland? We may never know.

Curiously enough, years later, another William Castle "gimmick" surfaced in Tomorrowland. In his last horror film, "Bug" (1975), Castle intended to use a device that would tickle the ankles of audience members every time cockroaches appeared on screen. The device, created but never actually used during the film's release, also bears a strong resemblance to the devices that tickled audience member's feet when rats appear on screen in the "Honey, I Shrunk the Audience!" attraction.

Let's not forget that one of Castle's early films was called "It's a Small World." Coincidence? Probably.

Lastly, there is another curious legend concerning the Haunted Mansion worth mentioning. Over the years, there have been rumors of an actual pet cemetery created by Cast Members near the dark ride's exit. Supposedly, there was an impromptu faux pet cemetery created by Cast Members for their own amusement, that inspired Imagineers to reinvent it on the Mansion's front lawn for the amusement of Guests waiting in line.

On a more light-hearted note, in an attempt to create merchandise for the "Haunted Mansion" attraction, the Walt Disney Company made little plush toys of Mickey Mouse dressed as a grave digger (or grave robber) with a shovel sewed to his hand. And, as if that weren't unseemly enough, Mickey is also smiling.

Speaking of inappropriate smiling, the grim, grinning ghosts that "come out to socialize," as the attraction's theme-song mentions, appear to (at least as presented in the "graveyard scene") actually be a collection of smiling, sociable spirits that spend their nights partying and singing.

These are not the typical doomed souls that are forced to wander the earth, or are bound to a specific location because of their sins, a family curse (Disneyland curse aside) or unfinished business. Thus, there are no unresolved issues with these ghosts. Once dead, we should all be so lucky. It seems that even in the after-life, Disneyland is the happiest place on Earth.

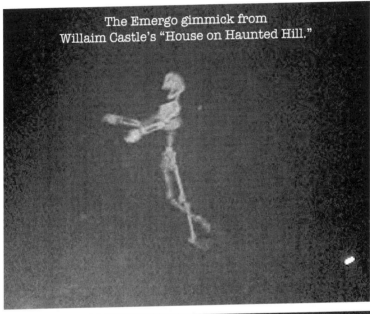

The Emergo gimmick from Willaim Castle's "House on Haunted Hill."

When the crypt doors creak
and the tombstones quake,
Spooks come out for a swinging wake!
Happy haunts materialize, and begin to vocalize.
Grim Grinning Ghosts come out to socialize!

Now don't close your eyes and don't try to hide,
For a silly spook may sit by your side.
Shrouded in a daft disguise,
they pretend to terrorize.
Grim Grinning Ghosts come out to socialize!

--- "Grim Grinning Ghosts" (Song)

...Come out to socialize...

Yes foolish mortals, it appears that this dark ride attraction is indeed visited by real ghosts. So much so that most Cast Members, who work the Haunted Mansion have a their own ghost stories based on their experiences at that attraction. Cast Members trading tales has become so common place that this gossipy activity is acknowledged by management

According to some Cast Members, the management allows (or at least looks the other way for) late night get-togethers after hours, inside the Haunted Mansion. There, in the closed attraction, Cast Members meet up to swap real ghostly tales and tell about their own personal spooky experiences while working at the Haunted Mansion like gathering around the campfire in summer camp to hear ghost stories.

It is said that management is aware of these impromptu story-telling sessions, and permits them to continue as long as two rules are strictly followed...

First, the organizers of these happenings can not advertise on social media or in-house flyers that one of these events is going to happen, it has to be entirely word of mouth only (by whispered communications during their normal shifts). Secondly, there can be no recordings or photographing of these events. The participants are only left with their memories. In essence, there can be no proof that these spooky meet-ups ever occurred on Disney property.

There are several prominent ghosts who have
retired here from creepy old crypts from all over
the world. Actually, we have 999 happy haunts
here, but there's room for a thousand.
Any volunteers? If you insist on lagging behind,
you may not need to volunteer.
The carriage that will carry you into the
moldering sanctum of the spirit world will
accommodate you and one or two loved ones.

--- Ghost Host, The Haunted Mansion

Happy Haunts...

Since writing "The Park After Dark: The Original Unauthorized Guide to the Happiest (Haunted) Place on Earth." many past and present Cast Members have approached me to share their own personal spooky ghost stories of the park, a wonderful by-product of having written about Disneyland folklore, and I greatly appreciate these interactions. Surprisingly, among their tales, a new Haunted Mansion ghost (or new to my research) has materialized.

It seems that Cast Members and even a few parkies (Disneyland fans), have seen something unusual while standing on the West side of the Haunted Mansion exterior facade, near the attraction's exit.

A little girl has been seen peeking out from one of the windows on the second floor. Needless to say, this backstage area is not easily accessible, and certainly children would not be permitted to be there.

Could this be a new ghost or could this be the same little girl seen in the ballroom sequence of the ride? Who knows. Either is possible. Another fun element to these tales is that similar versions of this girl appear in other sources.

Firstly, one of the original scripts of this attraction features a woman that would peek out from a second story window at guests approaching the Haunted Mansion. This gag was eventually realized at Snow White's Scary Adventure in Fantasyland with the audio animatronic Queen occasionally pulling back the curtain in the tower window.

Secondly, there was a TV special in the 1980s promoting Disneyland, where a group of tweens dare each other to go into the Haunted Mansion. One scared boy musters up the courage when a little girl accompanies him on the attraction. The fun however, ends when she suddenly disappears at the end of the ride. Of course as he walks away and looks back at the Haunted Mansions exterior facade, he sees her waving at him from the second floor balcony, before vanishing into thin air, implying she is one of the ghosts of the house.

Could people's knowledge of either one of these fictional ghosts seep into their subconscious so they think they see a girl on the second floor? Ufologists (those that study U.F.O. sightings) claim that sightings sometimes correspond with Unidentified Flying Objects in the pop culture (i.e. if a popular movie features triangle spaceships, sightings in real life of similar triangle ships increases). Coincidence?

There may be other factors at play here. Over the years I have heard so many ghost stories from Cast Members (again, thank you), and most of them center around a child, either a little boy or a little girl. There are just too many, that I have not chosen to write about them because the stories get repetitious, so instead I have, in the past, focused on ones that are a little more unusual, or have an interesting element connected to the tale.

However, Cast Members have seen phantom children in just about every attraction, in backstage areas, and other unexpected places, from a vanishing child running in the landscaped areas of Autopia to one on the tracks of Big Thunder Railroad. Then there are the yarns about disembodied giggling and sounds of little footsteps. There are just so many of these stories, that it makes you wonder if something else is happening.

Obviously, the brain is an amazing and complex organ, but sometimes it can play tricks on its user. Because it is almost impossible for the brain to interpret all the visual data coming in through our eyes, our brains take shortcuts. It actually only samples parts of what we "see" and then it fills in the gaps to create the overall "picture" based on past experiences. This skewed view of the world is thus always changing, because our brains are always sampling different information and therefore the gaps that need filling in shift around to make sense of the massive amounts of visual stimuli in the external world.

This is why you may not immediately see a lost item that is in plain sight, at least until your brain samples the area with the lost item. However, just as your brain can create an internal image that makes something in front of you appear to not be visible, it can also do the opposite and create something in front of you based on external cues that isn't really in front of you.

Could it be that since Cast Members at Disneyland are so hyper aware of children and safety that a shadow of something blowing in the window can cause the brain to fill in a gap with something they are accustomed to seeing even if it is out of context (such as a child in an unusual place) and as the brain gets more info and "looks closer' that something (a child) disappears.

Is this the reason some have seen a little girl ghost in a place a little girl can not be, and a place with no history of children, or reason for a haunting in such a spot? That's one possible scientific explanation for this recent phenomenon. Of course, its much more fun to believe that Disneyland, and the Haunted Mansion, are just overrun with ghostly children. If you were a child ghost, where would you haunt?

4

New Orleans is rich in music, history, good food,
and ghost stories. How else do you explain all
those rumors of a mansion being haunted? Folks
say the place is filled with 999 happy haunts, and
they're looking for someone to make it 1,000.
Go ahead and find out for yourself,
but don't expect me to go with ya!

--- "Captain" from the Mark Twain Riverboat

More
Momento Mori

Though from a story-telling point of view there has always been a question that "haunts" the Haunted Mansion. Namely, "Why are there 999 happy haunts?" It is never explained inside the ride why the house would be so haunted. Strangely, there is no imagined beginning for its life as a place for ghosts. That is, other than general invitations to ghosts to haunt this house. All the variations of the back stories invented during the development of this ride were abandoned and never really incorporated.

However, there is a strange implied reason for all the unrest at this popular Disneyland attraction. Just as this dark ride borrowed elements of the legends of the Myrtles Plantation, as mentioned earlier, it also connotes plantation life in general with its similar architecture, and its placement "up river" from "New Orleans" (coincidentally near where a plantation-themed restaurant once stood).

In addition, the other aspect to these places, which all have ghost stories, is that the lore is always rooted in their connection to the Civil War and/or slavery. If one looks closely enough, one can also see the subtle allusions to the Haunted Mansion's own ties to a "history of slavery" (even if it may be unintentional).

Other than the possible lynching reference at the start of the tour and the chained and shackled "ghost" at the end, the real clues of this "past" are found in the exterior architecture and the layout of the area.

The designs of plantations were based heavily on the greek style of architecture with its columns and rigid symmetry as if to demonstrate their control over the environment, and thus give the illusion of power. Incidentally, the ancient Greeks also had slaves. Contrasted against these (painted white) mansions, the slave quarters, on the other hand, were usually unpainted (brown) rustic structures usually near, and in the shadow of the plantation house.

One needs only to look at the style of architecture in the neighboring "Critter Country" to see an example of this rustic design. Could this adjacent "land" be the "slave village" meant to serve the "master" in the Haunted (plantation) Mansion? Now think about how the focal point of Critter Country is Splash Mountain, where the folk tales of (former slave) Uncle Remus are retold. Coincidence?

Also, consider that when standing at Disneyland's "Hub" (the center of the park's circular design), and choosing a destination while facing the various gateways, Critter Country is the only "land" in Disneyland that, to reach, one has to travel through two other "lands." First, you enter Adventureland, and starting in the jungles of Africa, you travel to the port of New Orleans (New Orleans Square), where you then go further up the river to the plantation, and finally reach your destination in the shacks of Critter Country where you find Uncle Remus' stories.

This trip through the "happiest place on Earth" could easily be interpreted as symbolic of the journey many Africans made to enslavement in the New World.

Incidentally, some people have suggested that the mysterious 33 marking the entrance to Disneyland's secret club in New Orleans Square has its origins in another secret club, the Klu Klux Klan (also known as the KKK). Interestingly, "K" is the 11th letter in the alphabet, and thus "KKK" (or three 11's) would equal 33. This is the same logic people use to explain Disneyland's address (1313 Harbor Blvd.) as representing MM for Mickey Mouse. Coincidence? So, perhaps this unmentioned subtext of slavery and racism in this area of the park is the contextual back-ground and "back story" that fuels the great disturbances of the tale presented inside the Haunted Mansion. Something to think about?

Additionally, also mentioned earlier, one of the initial concepts for the Haunted Mansion involved a former owner with a dark secret...

At the beginning of its development, when the attraction was supposed to be a walking tour through a haunted house, where a guide would lead a group through each room, informing the guests about the ghost stories of the house. The Haunted Mansion's supposed "legends" in that version of the attraction revolved around a tale concerning a "Captain Blood" (or "Captain Bloodmere" or "Captain Gore), who was the former owner of the mansion, and a pirate.

In one version of this backstory, it would be explained to the guests that this original owner was married to a woman that was the love of his life.

However, this well respected member of Southern society harbored the above mentioned dark secret that he hid from the world as well as his bride. Unbeknownst to everyone, his wealth, and thus his stature in the community, was built on lies.

He had amassed his fortune because of the double life he was leading. His alternate identity was that of a feared blood-thirsty pirate known on the high seas as Captain Blood/Bloodmere/Gore, which, again mentioned in an earlier chapter, this tale may have (or not) been based on an actual historical person.

This idea of a hero leading a darker double life had been mined many times at the Disney Studios, especially on TV with shows like Zorro, Elfego Baca, and The Scarecrow. By the time the Haunted Mansion was developed, it was a trope they were comfortable with and thus may have seemed like a good place to start.

Naturally, (according to your tour guide) the Captain's true love discovered his hidden past, and confronted him. When faced with his ugly reality and her new unfavorable perception of his true self, or perhaps to just keep this identity concealed, he flew into a rage and killed her.

In some version's her ghost then haunts him (her beating heart mimicking the imagined beating heart in Edgar Allen Poe's "Tell Tale Heart" that drives the main character to insanity). His bride's maddening haunting/taunting combined with the realization of the gravity of his actions (and the monster within himself), eventually drove the Captain to commit suicide. The tour guide further explains that this tragic romance is the basis for the things that go bump in the night in this once beautiful house.

Although this back story was scraped as the Haunted Mansion evolved in a different direction, fans are quick to point out that some remnants were left behind.

Nautical props as well as sea ferring allusions can still be seen inside the attraction, which subconsciously point to this abandon storyline. At least, that is the conventional wisdom about the Captain's eventual influence on this famous dark ride.

With that in mind, could it be possible that the omnipresent main character of Haunted Mansion, the Ghost Host (the attraction's narrator), is also one of these leftover facets of this forgotten pirate origin?

In the stretching room sequence, the Ghost Host's disembodied voice makes a possible reference to his suicide when insinuating that the guests are trapped in that room with no way out by stating "of course there's always my way... (as our attention is drawn to the hanging skeleton above), implying that he is that carcass, and that he hung himself to escape reality.

Could this be a reference to the Captain's suicide?

Many Haunted Mansion scholars think the Captain's plot may have possibly been intended as a way of linking the Haunted Mansion attraction with the Pirates of the Caribbean attraction since both were being developed at the same time and both are in close proximity to each other.

Fans are also quick to point out that there were a lot of elements that were recycled and appear in both rides such as audio animatronic figures that were just redressed to fit their different surroundings (also perhaps suggesting more double lives and alter egos).

There are many fan theories that have connected these two attractions (and Tom Saywer Island) to imagined pirate lore or to the famous pirate Jean Lafitte.

Even Lafitte's friend/co-conspirator and known pirate sympathizer, President Andrew Jackson has been implicated in some conspiracy theories. Imagining Jackson (and Jackson's ghost) is involved with the Haunted Mansion's history is especially fun considering that his actual ghost famously haunts the White House and other locations. There was even a 1942 screwball comedy called "The Remarkable Andrew" about Jackson's famous ghost. Is it a coincidence that the "Hatchet Man" portrait in the Haunted Mansion looks suspiciously like the Audio Animatronic figure of Andrew Jackson in the Hall of Presidents attraction in Florida's Walt Disney World? Yes, of course it's a coincidence, but its fun to think of the ramifications of Jackson depicted that way.

In this vein however, these is an odd pirate connection between these two beloved New Orleans Square attractions that most guests and fans seem to overlook, even if it is just a coincidence.

There is one big element of the Haunted Mansion's experience that makes a very surprising appearance in the Pirates attraction that may shed light on the Ghost Host's true (or possible) identity.

The Ghost Host narration was provided by character actor Paul Frees. That easily recognized (and often imitated) voice also comes out of the mouth of one of the characters in the neighboring pirate ride. Yes, that very familiar ghost's voice was also originally used for the flamboyant, red-beard auctioneer in the "take a wench for a bride" scene of Pirates of the Caribbean.

It should be mentioned that this particular scene has been removed, and reworked, or reimagined with a female pirate replacing the male auctioneer and no woman prisoners chained in bondage.

These "improvements" (or what imagineeers call "plus-ing" an attraction) have occurred over the decades in a perhaps misguided effort to make this subject matter more family friendly. Xavier "X" Atencio, one of the imagineers who created the ride commented on the changes by saying "This is Pirates of the Caribbean not the Boy Scouts of the Caribbean!"

Putting the changes (or plus-ing) aside for a moment, for almost half a century no one seemed to make much of the fact that the auctioneer and the Ghost Host had the same voice, and thus one could argue that the pirate auctioneer was the one delivering the Haunted Mansion's narration from beyond the grave. Is it a coincidence that the auctioneer was the only eloquent and gregarious character in the pirate ride?

Naturally its fun to read into this connection and surmise that the dark secret that the master of the Haunted Mansion (per the Captain Gore tale) keep hidden was that he was involved in the slave trade to the new world. One could even go a step further and say specifically the sex slave trade. Even by today's standards, sex trafficking is a shocking revelation that makes it very easy to imagine how the Captain Gore plot would play out. His wife stumbles on to this startling discovery, she accuses him of his role in this disgusting underground activity (worse than being just a pirate), and then subsequently she falls victim to his rage as that side of him that abuses women takes control. Not only does this woman dare to stand up to him, but dares to expose his unsavory side business.

Could the unnamed auctioneer actually be Captain Gore. An early conceptual drawing by Ken Anderson of the Captain Gore character featured red hair and a beard (not unlike the auctioneer) in a blue jacket almost identical to the auctioneer's blue jacket (and although not clearly visible to guests, the suicidal skeleton hanging in the Haunted Mansion is also wearing a blueish jacket. Coincidence?

Here is something else to consider, there is a sea ferring ghost that appears in the ballroom ("swinging wake") scene. He enters the festivities from outside through the hole in the wall created by the hearse. Because of his nautical costume, this ghostly transparent figure has been nicknamed by the fans "The Sea Captain."

The Sea Captain is generally thought to be one of those errant leftovers from the Captain Gore phase of the attraction. It's generally accepted that if this obscure ballroom character is meant to be Captain Gore, himself, then its simply an example of the former star of a previous storyline being cast aside and ending up as one of the minor miscellaneous ghosts as the show was rewritten, making him a possible footnote in the history of this attraction.

But, what if he is indeed actually the star of the show and no one realizes it? Curiously, the Ghost Host's narration stops just before we, the audience, are introduced to the Sea Captain. Is it a coincidence that The Ghost Host's last line before his "disappearance" is "The happy haunts have received your sympathetic vibrations and are beginning to materialize. They're assembling for a swinging wake, and they'll be expecting me: I'll see you all a little later." Then, as if on cue, the Sea Captain enters the "swinging wake."

One last thing that must be mentioned on this Ghost Host/auctioneer/Sea Captain subject. As stated before, the Haunted Mansion and Pirates of the Caribbean recycled audio-animatronic figures (and faces) by simply changing costumes and hair styles. Thus, the Sea Captain of the Haunted Mansion also appears in the Pirate of the Caribbean ride. Who is the Sea Captain in the other ride? The Auctioneer!

Is this all just a series of random coincidences? Maybe. But, its something to think about the next time you are inside the Haunted Mansion.

Before leaving this topic, there are a couple other points to bring up that have to do with the house, but may be connected to this concept of Captain Gore.

Firstly there is the oddity that the guests do not enter this attraction through the front door of the house. One enters through a side door past the formal entrance. Additionally, to get to this alternate opening, the line's cue directs people to the back corner of the house to walk along the porch to the front, and then continue on the porch to this side entrance. What is interesting about this forced side trip is that there is an old Southern saying about "walking on the porch." To go for a "walk on the porch" is a euphemism for romance. Could this odd detour that requires each guest to "walk on the porch" be a subtle way of implying that the attraction you are about to enter is about lovers?

Also, not only does one go into a side door, and is lead into a room that seems to stretch and lower, but the only way out (other than "my way") is a secret door that opens, revealing a dark hall, the portrait gallery.

The 2003 Haunted Manson movie portrayed this hall as a part of the maze of secret halls.

This introduces an interesting possibility. Are the areas that guests explore inside the Haunted Mansion meant to be secret passageways and hidden rooms?

First, one walks through the portrait gallery, whose only function appears to shuttle guests from the secret door in the stretching room to the large black room where "doom buggies" can be boarded. What is that cavernous back room with the giant spider web (and giant spider) supposed to be? Does it represent an underground cavern?

Many old mystery movies with a creepy mansion at the edge of a body of water (not unlike the adjacent "Rivers of America") feature a hidden waterway through a cave with a dock under the house that the villian(s) uses to quietly exit and enter the mansion. Could that be the original intention for this awkward room... Is it a launching point away from the house like the caverns at the beginning of the Pirates ride to link these two rides, and reenforce the Captain Gore concept? Coincidently, all the surrounding attractions (Pirates, Splash Mountain, Tow Sawyer Island, and even the Disneyland Railroad) all feature caves/caverns and waterways.

There appears to be some evidence that the Haunted Mansion was originally supposed to be a water ride like the famously flooded Houmas House Plantation. The Houmas House has some architectural similarities to the Haunted Mansion, and was featured in 1964's "Hush... Hush, Sweet Charlotte" (as well as 1989's "Fletch Lives" in a scene that parodies Disney's "Song of the South").

Did the Southern Gothic movie inspire anything in the ride? Did Imagineer's visit this once submerged house in their research tour of Louisiana? Is that why the "doom buggies seem to float around?

Do the secret passageways also imply hidden treasure and secret activities? As a side note, there was a 1974 TV special that featured a humorous musical number set inside Disneyland's Haunted Mansion. The idea being that two thieves (played by Ruth Buzzi and Sandy Ducan) were trying to rob the Haunted Mansion, implying that there were jewels and gold hidden somewhere inside the Mansion. Their search is cut short by ghosts that scare them away. They even sing and dance around a grotesque bust made for the show that vaguely looks like the Captain Gore of early concept art.

From there, the guests ride their buoyant vehicles up a set of stairs into a hall to a room where a man is trapped in a coffin... Is this man being tortured? Has some unseen person nailed him into this wooden death trap? If so, is this a secret room where these kind of nefarious activities can take place? And who would be so cruel? Could it be the actions of a murderous pirate? Could all the ghosts that haunt this house be other victims?

Next, guests travel down a hall with many doors. Could these doors lead to other parts of the house, or ways to secretly reenter the house. Coincidentally, in Walt Disney World. Below the Magic Kingdom, there is a Utility Corridor (the "Utilidore") lined with doors not unlike this scene, so Cast Members can seemlessly appear or disappear from hidden entry points around the park, gliding to/from this underground hall to/from just about anywhere in the park as needed.

In Florida, there is even a door in this utilador that leads to stairs that ascend to another door, which is one of the doors in the Magic Kingdom's Haunted Mansion in this very scene. It's almost surreal.

This idea of a network of secret tunnels under or inside the Haunted Mansion (which also appears in the 1972 Haunted Mansion board game) could explain two conceptual mysteries about the attraction that fans have pondered for decades.

First, there is no way this ride's "floor plan" could actually exist inside the house we see from the outside as we enter the attraction, unless it uses secret tunnels that extend underground and beyond the house (perhaps into the adjacent berm).

Secondly, there is the issue of the exterior of the seen house not even remotely resembling the exterior of the house guests exits when entering the graveyard scene at the rides finale. This incongruity could be explained that perhaps, via secret passageways, the doom buggies have entered a nearby (or adjacent) house that is connected by these hidden tunnels. Clearly, this is all just speculation, but it's fun to apply this logic on the house's illogical properties.

Fans have tried to explain these issues by claiming that Guests, by way of the doom buggies, are actually entering, and traveling through, the spirit realm and thus the rules of logic and physics do not apply inside the house, which explains the sign at the end of the ride announcing the "return to the living." If true, that would mean that the guests (contrary to a theory discussed in a previous chapter) die at the beginning of the show to make this possible.

That would also mean that the hanging skeleton might represent ones own death. Clearly, the secret passageway/hidden room theory makes more sense.

Even if you don't accept this idea, one must admit the seance room with Madam Leota feels different...

Of all the scenes and areas inside this attraction this room, with its open space and darkness, and with no discernible details or fixtures (not unlike the loading area) does feel like a secret room. Its as if you have wandered out of that hall into the shadows and into a hidden place that few people get a chance to see. And just as seemlessly, the guests slip out of that room into the ballroom, where the "swinging wake" occurs. However, there is a strange voyeuristic feeling about this scene. You are not part of the party, but are observing it from the shadows of a secret area.

Again there is that strange sensation that you are passing through from a hidden balcony that allows you to see into the room, but "they" can't see you.

From there, the next room (and final room), is the Attic. Again, one slides through the darkness into this room, which could simply be an attic as many believe, or it could be a chamber that is only discovered if you know how to navigate these back ways and find the hidden entry. Could this room be the proverbial closet where the house's so-called skeletons are kept, the dark locked away secrets of the former inhabitants. Remember, this room has the nautical artifacts.

This room has also been changed semi-recently to support a new "Constance" storyline with "remnants" of a "black widow" type female who has murdered a string of spouses.

This again was another attempt by imagineers to "plus" the attic scene, and remove the glorious ambiguity of this attraction that contributed to the mystery that fascinated generations.

If we put aside the new "Constance" elements, and remember the attic the way it used to be, its easy to imagine how the Captain Gore storyline played out in this house. Could this be the room where the bride discovered her husband's pirate past (or present)? Is this where she confronted him, and where he killed her? In those early versions of the Haunted Mansion's supposed backstory featuring the secret life of piracy, the tale not only involved him murdering her to hide the truth, but him also hiding her body as well somewhere in the house.

Could this "hidden room" be where he hid the body? Perhaps in one of those trunks. Is this why her ghost was here eternally confronting Guests just like she confronted him?

Also note that, per the revealing vision at the beginning of this adventure, in the stretching room, the Ghost Host hung himself above, in the attic of the house. Is this why he killed himself there, because it was the same room that he killed her, and thus he was driven to this final action of taking his life because of her ghost haunting him in that room, taunting him with that echoing beating heart.

Thus, the story comes full circle, from the glimpse, or foreshadowing in the first room (the stretching room) to the conclusion in the last room (the attic). But wait, there is an epilogue. Even in death, the tragic Captain can not escape her ghost.

The bride appears one last time in the crypt at the very end of the attraction as if to say, that even in death his bride haunts him for eternity. There is no solace for him in the spirit realm.

Yes, even though the conventional wisdom is that the original Captain Gore yarn was abandoned with only traces leftover in the ride as it exists today, that might not be the case (or rather casket).

One could look at this ride and easily interpret that the Captain Gore legend is still present and drives the contextual story of this attraction. From walking along the porch to enter the building to seeing the bride as you exit the building, and all the secret rooms (and secrets) in between. Captain Gore and his ill deeds have left their mark on this house, scaring it forever.

Just something to think about the next time you pass through Disneyland's Haunted Mansion.

"Have you ever seen a haunted house? You know the kind I mean. That old dark house that's usually at the end of a dimly lit street. The owner's haven't been seen for years; no one really knows why.... It's a house that people avoid walking past at night. Strange sounds come from within the walls, and it's said that eerie lights have been seen in the attic window and in the graveyard at the side of the house. Our Story revolves around this mysterious mansion"

--- Narrator, "The Story and Song from the Haunted Mansion" LP Album

"The Sea Captain"

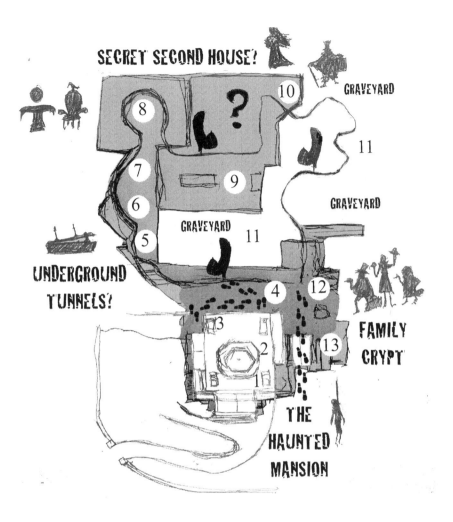

1.) Foyer (Entrance)
2.) Stretching Room
3.) Portrait Corridor
4.) Load Area
5.) Endless Hallway
6) Conservatory
7.) Corridor of Doors

8.) Seance Circle
9.) Grand Hall
10.) Attic
11.) Graveyard
12.) Crypt (Load Off)
13.) Little Leota (Exit)

The following chapter
has been reprinted from the book
"Spirits with Spirits: Los Angeles Vol. 3"
by
Richard Carradine

(for more info go to page #99)

Spirits with Spirits

The recreation center known today as The Pickwick Bowl, in the 1940s, was just a trailer park with a community swimming pool. Despite the innocuous slogan "For 'fun in the sun' meet me at the Pickwick Pool," this small body of water had more than its share of scandal and urban legends. Not only did a "squeaky clean" teen-age celebrity reputedly get caught exposing himself to the other swimmers (leading to his firing at Disney Studios, and essentially the end of his career), but for some strange reason the pool area seemed to attract fatal injuries as children died from drownings and diving board accidents. Safety concerns were most likely the reason the pool was eventually filled in with dirt (creating the Pickwick Gardens).

In 1949, the adjacent property was developed into the Pickwick Drive-In, which subsequently became famous as a filming location, because of its proximity to many studios (including the Walt Disney Studios). Anytime a movie of TV show required a drive-in theater, more often than not, it was the Pickwick.

Most likely because of the neighboring theater's success, in 1958, the Pickwick Gardens was paved over to make room for other entertainment/recreation venues. The owners began construction on a new bowling alley and ice rink complex. However, they may have built over the old "death magnet" pool at that site, but apparently they didn't get rid of its dark influence.

"Pickwick"

Employees have confidentially claimed that many more people have died (accidentally) on the ice rink. It should be noted that the management denies this macabre rumor. Strangely, all the deaths that seem to swarm around the premises have nothing to do with Pickwick Bowl's ghost story.

The employees claim (and again the management denies) that the ghost of a former member of their staff haunts the upstairs office. Papers and other objects have been seen sliding forcefully across the desk for no apparent reason, as well as the door to that office seems to close by itself, or unseen forces. Because of the location of the haunting and type of paranormal activity, it is assumed that the resident spirit is a former employee.

That said, this recreation center has another claim to fame in the Southern Californian ghost culture. Pickwick Bowl is said to have served as the inspiration for one of the audio-animatronic "happy haunts" from Disneyland's Haunted Mansion. There used to be a sign in front of this leisure complex that featured a caricature of "Pickwick," the Dickens character (and this establishment's mascot). It seems that Imagineers that would commute to work at WED enterprises (now Walt Disney Imagineering) just a few blocks away decided to pay tribute to the cheerful fellow on the sign they passed everyday to and from home. Thus, in the ballroom scene of Disneyland's Haunted Mansion, a ghost hanging from a chandelier (also known by the name "Pickwick") holding a glass of booze was created to match the one on the Pickwick Bowl sign.

So today, one can visit this establishments's bar and toast this ghost, who eternally holds his glass in the air in the toasting position. BOOoooowling anyone!

The following chapter
has been reprinted from the book
"Dark Rides in the Sunshine: The Haunted
Amusement Parks of Southern California"
by
Richard Carradine

(for more info go to page #98)

The Disneyland of Death

Although technically this graveyard was open for business in 1906, it officially didn't become a visitor-friendly "memorial park" until 1917. This is easily one of the weirdest (haunted) tourist attractions in Los Angeles, which obviously is really saying something.

In 1912, Hubert Lewright Eaton began working here, selling plots, at this dreary grave-yard in the new town of Tropico (now called Glendale) when he came up with the revolutionary idea of selling "before needed" plots (as in buying your own grave while you're still living). He made so much money on his commissions, he was able to buy the property, and become the new boss.

This visionary man had even more big ideas for this little cemetery in Glendale. For instance, he wanted to remove the sad stigma associated with such monuments of death, so he eliminated the tombstones, recreated famous churches from around the world, installed exact replicas of masterpieces of art, displayed historical artifacts, built auditoriums for shows, and built the world's largest gates (bigger than Buckingham Palace's). Lastly, he removed the dreaded "c word" (cemetery), and changed the name of this final resting place to the more pleasant-sounding "Memorial Park."

Eaton saw absolutely no reason why families shouldn't want to spend the day exploring the grounds of this open-air environment.

Why not have a picnic on the final resting place of your relatives? How about a friendly game of catch in a graveyard? There's grass and fountains like any other parkland. Better still, what about bringing your (living) relatives from out of town there to do some local sight-seeing? He dreamed that one day it may even be a tourist destination for those vacationing in Southern California. His idea was that you would visit Hollywood, then Disneyland and then, of course, this cemetery.

In 1948, Evelyn Waugh's wrote the satirical book, "The Loved One: An Anglo-American Tragedy" (which later spawned a cult film staring Robert Morse also called "The Loved One"), which lampooned the "death industry." It featured a fictional theme park-like cemetery that had statues wired for sound, a souvenir shop with grave-yard post cards, and a costumed actor portraying Abraham Lincoln interacting with guests. The story was obviously based on Glendale's Forest Lawn, which had all of the before-mentioned items.

When the book came out, Eaton was not amused. His "memorial" empire was serious business. Even still, the oddness of his approach caused it to be lovingly referred to by outsiders as the "Disneyland of Death" (even back in Walt Disney's time). Like Disneyland, Forest Lawn is divided in to "lands," has story-book architecture, historical displays, attractions, a theater, actors portraying walk-around characters, atmospheric music from hidden speakers, themed-trash cans sculpted to look like tree stumps, and most importantly a steady flow of bewildered tourists.

Given its proximity to Walt Disney Studios, one can only surmise what influence it may have had on the famous theme park being developed a few miles away.

Not surprisingly, it is also the site of where everyone claims Disney's cremated remains are kept. Despite dubious rumors that his frozen body is elsewhere, Disney's grave in the "Garden of Freedom" is probably the most visited final resting place in the memorial park. There are those that also claim that Walt's ghost protects this site. Although no one has actually seen Disney's ghost here, the claim is that he will curse and avenge any visitor that may vandalize, disrupt, or remove a souvenir while visiting his final resting place. Aside from angering his ghost, it is said there is hidden surveillance equipment here, so don't try anything.

Also, not surprisingly, the place is said to be haunted by ghosts that roam the grounds and some of the subterranean areas. In recent years, paranormal investigators have claimed that Michael Jackson's troubled spirit has been seen near his crypt, which is in a part of the cemetery not easily accessed by the visiting public. Even more expected, it is said to be haunted by the memorial park pioneer himself, Dr. Hubert Eaton.

At the top of the property, like the biblical "city upon a hill," sits a complex of buildings, including a surprisingly good museum with changing exhibits, and a massive theater, built specifically to exhibit an enormous 195-ft x 45-ft, panoramic painting, which is said to be the largest mounted religious painting in the world. The work is titled "The Crucifixion," and it was originally intended to be exhibited at the St. Loius Exposition of 1904, but a building to showcase it was never built.

It was conceived to be seen in-the-round, where the canvas wrapped around the viewers, creating a 360 degree view, and thus placing the observer in the middle of this famous biblical event. The artist, Jan Styka, didn't have the funds to bring it home to Poland, so he left it behind. It was eventually bought by Eaton (sight unseen) and shipped to Glendale.

Although well worth the visit, clearly it doesn't draw the crowds to justify such a large auditorium, meaning, much of the time, most of the seats are empty. There is one seat that gets a little more use than the others though, even if it is reserved for a ghost. Employees have secretly claimed that they see Eaton's spirit sitting back and enjoying the light show and recorded narration that accompanies this artistic marvel, only to evaporate into the air when the houses lights come on at the end. It seems even in death he finds solace staring into this masterpiece's beauty.

Hurry back!
Hurry back!
Be sure to bring your death certificate,
if you decide to join us.
Make final arrangements now!
We've been dying...
to have you...

--- Little Leota, The Haunted Mansion

"The happy haunts have received your sympathetic vibrations and are beginning to materialize. They're assembling for a swinging wake, and they'll be expecting me. I'll see you all a little later..."

--- Ghost Host, The Haunted Mansion

Ectoplasm Punch

25% bourbon
15% sugar
20% water
10% creme de mint
15% frozen lemonade
15% frozen limeade

Combine ingredients
3 drops of green food coloring
Add maraschino cherries

"It ain't over til the fat lady sings."

--- **Origin of the saying unknown
(popularized by Don Meredith)**

Afterword

While my mother was pregnant, my grandmother and my mother consulted a Ouija Board to have the moldering sactum of the spirit world divine a name for me, the unborn child. The name that the playful ghosts spelled out was... D-A-G-M-A-C-L-A-M-O-G-O

My Grandmother nick-named me with the abbreviated version "Dagmac." Needless to say, I grew up in a (haunted) household surrounded by believers of the occult. The supernatural was just the natural. My grandmother consulted psychics through most of her life, and my mother believed she processed acute psychic abilities, a trait that unfortunately was not passed down to me. Before I was born, my parents engaged in pallor games with friends, where an object would be hidden, and my mother, using only her psychic powers, would describe its location. She even taught classes on how one can improve their own natural intuition. Between my mother and her "sensitive" friends, stories of the spirits and haunted places was a staple of my childhood.

Thus, it should not surprise anyone that Disneyland's Haunted Mansion is my favorite ride, not just at Disneyland, but anywhere. However, it is not just my predisposed fondness of all things spooky that appeals to me, which it does mostly, it's a certain level of pride, seeing the influence of one of my ancestors reflected in this famous attraction.

Let me explain. My great grandmother, Ernestine Schumann-Heink, has a very indirect connection to this attraction. Although, her talent as an opera singer has been largely forgotten, her influence on pop culture is easily recognized. It has been said that because of her power house performance in a 1896 production of Wagner's "Gotterdammerung" (part of Wagner's epic opera "Der Ring des Nibelungen" aka "The Ring Cycle,"), she became a star and made this opera famous. Thus, her image as in that role (ample figure, Viking-esque winged helmet, long blonde braids) has become synonymous with that opera, and opera, itself, and a short hand in depicting the cliche opera singer. Her "look" has been imitated and parodied over the decades since she donned that now familiar outfit.

But, perhaps one of the most enduring tributes to her is the ghostly "Opera Singer" that appears in the Haunted Mansion's graveyard. It has also been said that her notoriety in that role may be the inspiration for the expression "It ain't over till the fat lady sings..." Even if unintentional, I think it's fitting that the rotund singer appears at the end of the ride.

Just as I hope this fun book changes the way you look at this Disney attraction, hopefully you will look at that opera singer a little differently too.

Dagmaclamogo Martin
Hollywood, 2019

Note: Ernestine Schumann-Heink (the original Viking helmeted opera singer) is said to haunt another amusement park in Southern California.
(for more info go to page #98)

"The Opera Singer"

Did you enjoy your visit? I told you, you would not be harmed. Thank you for spending some time with us; come back again. Bring your friends if they'll believe the story you'll tell. I have to go now, it's midnight.
Pleasant dreams...

**---Ghost Host, "The Story and Song
from the Haunted Mansion" LP Album**

"We spirits haunt our best in gloomy darkness,
so remember no flash pictures please."
---The Haunted Mansion

PICTURE TIPS
for capturing
GHOSTS at Disneyland

1.) Be respectful of other Guests and rules.

2.) Press button when you feel a temperature change.

3.) Frame the picture with an object to provide scale.

4.) Hold camera steady as you press the button.

5.) Snap your picture during a quiet moment.

6.) Call out a question before photographing.

7.) Point the camera at known haunted subjects.

8.) Photograph dark environments.

9.) Photograph the subject twice.

10.) Record time of photograph.

11.) Bring extra batteries.

12.) Try a red filter.

13.) Have fun.

Note: The type of camera you use, as well as if you use the flash or not, is not important. Strange phenomena can be captured regardless of these factors. However, specific anomalies have been known to favor certain technical aspects. Experiment for yourself to see what works best for you.

A CHILLING CHALLENGE:

Now that you have read a sampling of the ghosts stories people have told about the Haunted Mansion over the years... If you want, you can explore this lore further? There are a few simple ways the budding amateur ghost-hunter can. As a starting point, take the knowledge obtained from this guide, and see what other information (and enjoyment) can be obtained while visiting the "Happiest Place on Earth."

Next time you're at the Haunted Mansion, take the **"V.I.P."** Tour. That is... **V**isit, **I**nvestigate, and **P**hotograph (or **V.I.P.**, for short).

First, visit the supposed haunted areas of the attraction. Experience them. Take note of your feelings. Keep your eyes open for anything unusual.

Secondly, investigate these places. Talk to the Cast Members. See if they have (or are willing to tell) any stories. If they have a new one, or variation of one, jot it down in the "Notes" section following these pages. (Also, please send any new information to us, using the "Ghost Post [Card]" found in the back of this guide.)

Thirdly, take lots of pictures, and scrutinize them for any strange anomalies that appear in the photos (that were seemingly not present at the time the picture was taken). Although, there are many devices one can buy to try and capture evidence of a ghost, cameras are generally the simplest, easiest and most inconspicuous while in the park. Enjoy!

Haunted Mansion's
HAUNTED AREA CHECK-LIST

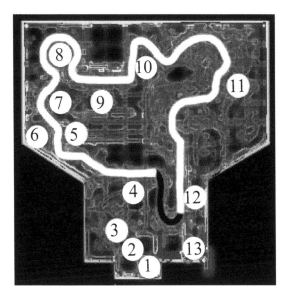

	V	I	P
1.) Foyer (Entrance)	☐	☐	☐
2.) Stretching Room	☐	☐	☐
3.) Portrait Corridor	☐	☐	☐
4.) Load Area	☐	☐	☐
5.) Endless Hallway	☐	☐	☐
6) Conservatory	☐	☐	☐
7.) Corridor of Doors	☐	☐	☐
8.) Seance Circle	☐	☐	☐
9.) Grand Hall	☐	☐	☐
10.) Attic	☐	☐	☐
11.) Graveyard	☐	☐	☐
12.) Crypt (Load Off)	☐	☐	☐
13.) Little Leota (Exit)	☐	☐	☐

Notes

Notes

Please email any new discoveries to...
ghoulahq@live.com

(Clockwise from top right:
The author, "Mr. One Way,"
"Disco Debbie," and "?")

Richard Carradine (Author): As a result of his paranormal interests, in 2006, Mr. Carradine founded GHOULA (a social club for Southern Californian ghost-enthusiasts) to preserve the haunted history of Los Angeles and celebrate that lore through events and publications. In addition to chronicling these tales and lecturing to historical societies and other groups, Mr. Carradine leads ghost tours and hosts spooky meet-ups that also emphasize the city's dark past. Because of his unique knowledge in local phantom folklore, he consults for TV programs, and has been profiled by NPR and the BBC. The LA Weekly has even declared him "The Best Host to Toast a Ghost" in their "Best of LA" issue, which also said he is responsible for the "Best Ghostly Gatherings" and "Best Weirdo Tours."

If you have seen a ghost at Disneyland, or have a different version of one of the stories in this book, please fill out this post card, and email the info to ghoulahq@live.com. Thank you.

Date: Time: Location:

Please Describe Experience:

GHOULA PRESS

Email:
ghoulahq@live.com

Please use the other side of this post card to draw exactly what was experienced.

GHOST POST (CARD)

Use this side to draw exactly what was experienced.

Also from GHOULA Press!

MORE Disneyland ghost stories!

Also from GHOULA Press!

MORE amusement park ghost stories!

Also from GHOULA Press!

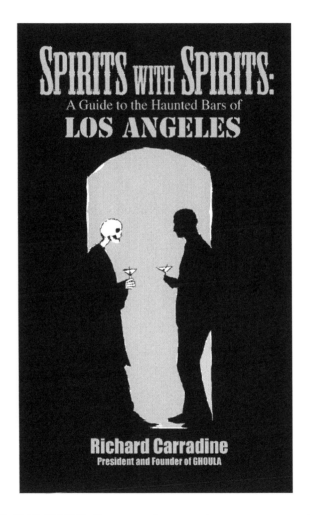

MORE bar/restaurant ghost stories!

Meet Walt Disney's Ghost!

Look directly and continuously at the four dots on "Uncle Walt's" nose, below the eyes, while counting slowly up to 33. Then, immediately look at a blank wall, or into the sky - and YOU WILL SEE an image of his ghost appear before your eyes.

45113000R00061

Printed in Poland
by Amazon Fulfillment
Poland Sp. z o.o., Wrocław